MAKING YOUR OWN
PAPERCRAFT GIFTS

MELANIE WILLIAMS

NH
NEW
HOLLAND

First published in the UK in 1995 by
New Holland (Publishers) Ltd
Chapel House, 24 Nutford Place,
London W1H 6DQ

ISBN 1 85368 522 4 (hbk)
1 85368 523 2 (pbk)

Editor Coral Walker
Art director Jane Forster
Design assistant Sarah Willis
Photographer Shona Wood
Illustrator Terry Evans
Calligrapher David Harris

Phototypeset by Ace Filmsetting Ltd, Frome,
Somerset
Originated by HBM Print Pte Ltd, Singapore
Printed and bound in Singapore by Kyodo Printing
Co (Pte) Ltd

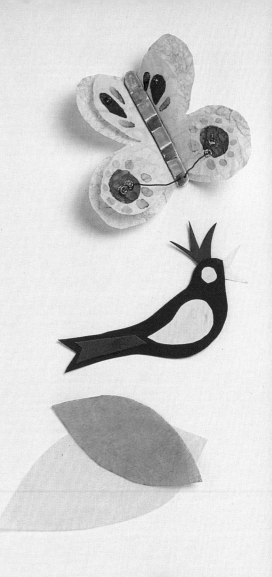

Contents

Introduction

We all come into contact with paper every day, whether it is simply packaging, money or for communication purposes, yet we rarely consider its qualities, how it is made, or the many ways in which it can be used and manipulated.

To give you some idea of the amazing versatility of paper and its potential, in this book I explain clearly how to make a wonderful variety of gifts and practical items, using paper of varying colours, textures and qualities.

The book is divided into chapters covering different types of projects you may wish to embark on, whether you want to make a gift, work with a child or make something for children, make up decorations, or simply create something new and special for yourself. The projects involve various techniques from simple paper cutting to more complex quilling.

The chapters include *Gifts and giftwrap*, which explains how to make your own wrapping papers, gift tags, a presentation box and greetings cards. The *For the home* chapter covers a number of practical household items, such as a bowl, dressing table set, lampshade and roller blind. This chapter also explores a wide range of techniques, such as quilling, decoupage and papier mâché. In the chapter *For children* I have included a number of projects which can be made by, with, or for children. These projects focus on bold, bright colours and simple techniques such as collage, stencilling and gluing.

Everything starts with the fundamental chapter *How to begin*, which covers techniques and processes that occur in the projects that follow, such as basic construction, paper arts like quilling, origami and papier mâché, and decorative procedures: stencilling, decoupage and various paint techniques. This section also

offers a comprehensive guide to what tools, equipment and materials are required and how to use them to their greatest advantage.

The choice and variety of papers now available from hobby, art, craft and specialist paper shops is vast. Machine-made papers can be bought in a wide range of colours and finishes, but also look out for the more unusual handmade papers. These wonderfully tactile papers come from every corner of the world and are sometimes made from strange base materials such as bark, leaves, flowers and grass.

I have tried to incorporate as many different types of paper in the following projects as possible, but have taken into consideration that some more obscure papers may be quite difficult to obtain, so have avoided suggesting their use; although if you have access to more unusual and exciting papers then I hope you will feel free to use them.

At the beginning of each project is a list of materials you will require, including recommended papers and decorative finishes. Although I may suggest certain colours and types of paper, once you are more familiar with the differences (ie weight, strength and translucency), you may like to introduce your own ideas, or employ other methods found through experimentation, or from other sources. This especially relates to the decoration of the roller blind, papier mâché bowl, nest of boxes and wrapping paper. Most projects also offer variations and tips which can be helpful to note before undertaking them. Where possible, I have avoided using equipment or materials which you may find expensive or difficult to obtain. Most projects use basic equipment and materials, such as papers, card, glue, paints, inks, a craft knife, scissors and tape. It is likely that you will be able to find most of what you need around the home.

Chapter 1
How to begin

Most of the materials and equipment used in the following projects are easy to find and inexpensive to buy. You can begin with virtually no outlay at all, using photocopy paper, newspaper, flour, water, poster paints, scissors and glue; all items you may well have already in your home. Specialised materials, such as handmade papers, can be a little more expensive, but the pleasure of choosing them and incorporating them into your designs is well worth the outlay.

Many of the techniques featured are straightforward and clearly explained in each project. However, basic methods – such as decoupage, papier mâché and quilling – are explained in this chapter as a useful and handy reference.

> **Note:** *Instead of throwing away packaging from goods you buy, look to see if any paper can be rescued and stored ready for a paper project. Paper scraps take up little space in a portfolio or large envelope and can be fun to sort through later for gift ideas and inspiration.*

Materials
Papers

The basic material in every project throughout the book is paper. The variety of strengths, textures and weights available is massive and its versatility makes it a great material with which to work.

I have selected particular papers for certain projects because of specific qualities they have, ie tissue paper for lightness, brown paper for durability and its natural appearance, sugar paper for its textured, grainy surface.

Although, at the beginning of each project I may suggest using a specific paper, there is no reason, so long as you are aware of the individual qualities of each paper type, why you cannot use an alternative. This will also result in something that is original to you and therefore all the more exciting.

Before embarking on any projects in this book, do browse around your local art and craft shop and see what there is available. Also retain paper scraps which occur around the home such as paper bags, old wrapping paper, magazines, tissue paper, etc. These are easy to store and can all go towards creating something special.

Sugar paper: Very absorbent paper with an interesting grainy appearance. Medium weight, available in a good choice of colours, this paper has a natural quality.

Newsprint: The best choice for papier mâché projects as it has excellent absorbency. Avoid any newspapers which have shiny coatings or finishes. It also costs nothing, as such!

Handmade papers: These come as both plain and highly textured papers, ie they have grass, flowers, glitter etc, incorporated into them. These are ideal for making little books or stationery, or where a special decorative finish is required. These papers are usually quite expensive.

Tissue paper: A lightweight, translucent paper in a wide range of colours. Tissue paper is not very strong, so use it for a decorative element or to reveal a light source (for example, a lampshade, see page 48).

Layout paper: This lightweight, yet strong, paper is used by art students or graphic designers. It is not adversely affected when wet and therefore responds well to the application of paint or ink washes. It is also quite good for tracing through.

Brown paper: A strong paper with a matt or shiny side which is mainly used for wrapping parcels. However, its natural appearance, especially when combined with twines and coloured papers, can make it a successful paper for some projects. It is also very inexpensive to buy.

Watercolour paper: This thick, grainy paper is very absorbent and will respond well with watery paint or ink washes, as it will not buckle, warp or shrink. It is sold for watercolour painting and is quite expensive. However, its almost handmade quality makes it an excellent decorative paper in its own right.

Crêpe paper: A lightweight paper that 'stretches'. It is ideal for making paper flowers and gift wrapping. It can also be quite strong. Available in a wide range of colours, you can achieve a number of quite interesting effects when you introduce water to its surface.

Paper is available in such a wide range of colours, textures, weights and qualities, that it can be difficult to make a choice. Although a specific paper is usually recommended in each project, a great deal of fun can be had by experimenting with something you have selected yourself.

Adhesives

PVA glue: The majority of projects require an adhesive of some sort. I frequently refer to PVA glue. It is a strong, clear-drying paper glue. It can also be watered down if you wish to cover a larger area and make the paper cling neatly to another surface. To spread the glue easily, cut a piece of card about 5 cm (2 in) square and use it to apply the glue evenly and quite thinly on to the paper, avoiding wrinkles and bubbles.

When diluting PVA glue, mix it with water to a ratio of 1:1.

A solution of PVA glue can also stiffen fine papers when applied in a thin coat, see page 48, for example.

Spray adhesive: This type of adhesive – used by professional designers and artists – is ideal for applying a neat, even layer of glue on to a surface, as the aerosol disperses a mist of adhesive particles. You do not require much of this glue; but make sure you always use it with a large scrap of paper underneath in a well-ventilated room, as it is strong-smelling and very sticky. Another advantage of this adhesive is that it eliminates wrinkling and warping because it is solvent-based.

Tape: Tape is used in a variety of projects for holding things in position and for making up boxes. Clear sticky tape can be used, but where you want to paint, or if the tape is likely to be visible, use masking tape, because it is more like the paper itself, and colours can be applied to it more satisfactorily.

Gum arabic: This glue comes in a solid lump, which is then mixed with water to make a glue solution. It is also available already mixed. It is the ideal medium to use on tissue papers as it causes the paper to shrink and become stiff and taut.

Decorative materials

Paints: Paint is used in many of the projects. I have used simple poster paints, the type available in little pots. An alternative to these are gouache paints and watercolours, or most other water-based paints. However, avoid acrylics as these are not that sympathetic with fine papers.

I also suggest coating a number of the pieces in a layer of white emulsion paint. This is an ideal primer for papier mâché and any surface which is to be decorated with paint or collage.

Inks: Coloured inks are very successful when used on fine papers. I have suggested using them watered down on damp, creased layout paper, which creates a beautiful, delicately toned, crinkled paper that resembles leather.

Gold rubbing paste: Although you can use gold inks and paints, they are sometimes very disappointing and look no more interesting than a yellowy-brown paint. But gold paste, which comes in a tube or tub normally used by picture framers, gently rubbed on edges or scuffed across a textured surface, will add life and sparkle to the piece to which it is being applied. It comes in a number of tones, like copper, and is also known as gilt wax. It is sold in art shops.

Equipment
Cutting tools
In most of the projects, you will require a cutting tool, such as scissors or a scalpel.

When using a craft knife, always keep it filled with a sharp, fresh blade; this makes an accident more unlikely, because you need to place less pressure on it to cut. It is also wise to cut against a metal ruler or a safety ruler with a ridge down the middle.

Cut on to either a cutting mat (available from craft shops) or a scrap piece of board. When cutting, always tilt the knife slightly away from your fingers, just in case it should slip. It is also better to make a number of gentle cuts, rather than one hard one. A scalpel is more suitable for some projects as it is less bulky and more pointed.

Scissors are another vital piece of equipment. Most of the time a simple, average-sized pair of sharp scissors is fine, but it a good idea to have a smaller pair for tiny corners and little details. Pinking shears are useful when a decorative, zigzag edge is required.

If you have access to a desk-top guillotine, this is useful for cutting large pieces of paper into smaller pieces, as the cut is clean all the way along the edge.

Another handy tool for making neat holes in paper and card, in projects such as the gift tags, is a stationery hole punch.

Drawing aids
It is often necessary for you to trace templates and draw outlines or measurements, so a variety of sharpened pencils is essential, as well as tracing paper and an eraser.

Techniques
Block printing

This method involves gathering objects which will produce an interesting pattern, ie sponges, cardboard tubes, cotton reels, corks and halved vegetables. The paint is applied to the object, which is then pressed on to the paper.

Another more professional way of making a block print pattern is to use textile printing blocks.

Potato cuts are fun and a very simple and effective way to apply a repeat pattern. Simply make a neat cut across the middle of a medium or large potato, wash away the starch and pat dry with kitchen paper or a clean tea towel. Draw a design on to the cut potato and use a sharp knife or scalpel to cut away the potato around the design. You are left with a raised image which can be used again and again.

Crinkled paper technique

In a number of the projects, such as the mobile and the butterflies, I have suggested using layout paper, creased and washed with watered-down inks. To do this, screw up a piece of layout paper into a ball and then unscrew it and lay it out flat. Apply a wash of watered-down ink, using a large soft brush, hang up and leave to dry.

Stencilling

This traditional method of decorating is frequently used on textiles and walls, but can work extremely well on paper. I have included it in a number of projects, such as the nest of boxes (on page 74) and the tablecloths (on page 52). You will require oiled stencil card to do this successfully; it is non-absorbent so allows you to use it repeatedly. Thin card or acetate will also work, but these materials are less durable.

You can buy pre-cut stencils, but I have provided templates for you to use in several of the projects. Use a very sharp scalpel to cut away the stencil, so that you get a clear image. It is also a good idea to tape the stencil to the paper you are working on.

You will require a stencil brush to apply the paint; the brush is very stiff and the bristles are short. Use a small amount of paint on the brush, but keep it quite thick to avoid any seepage under the stencil. Hold the brush upright and work the paint on to the paper with a dabbing motion. Remove the stencil carefully so that you do not smudge it. Before you reposition the stencil, be sure no paint has seeped to the underside of the card. If it has you might need to touch up the design when dry. You will also need to wipe the underside of the card before repositioning it.

Sponging

You can use a sponge as a way of applying paint to create your stencil in the same way as the brush, or you can use it to create a dappled effect. Small natural sponges are the most successful for this method; they can be obtained from chemists or art shops.

Spraying and spattering

These are simple methods and are ideal for decorating a large area like wrapping paper. The paint should be mixed to a thin consistency and used with a spray diffuser. The consistency of the paint affects the size of the spray. Alternatively, you can spatter the paint from a stiff brush or toothbrush. Hold the bristles upwards and draw either your finger or a piece of stiff card or a blunt knife across the bristles towards yourself, so the paint spatters on to the paper you wish to decorate. Any amount of colours or layers can be applied.

> *Note:* Be ready to experiment with an assortment of decorative techniques; mix and match say sponging with finished papier mâché, or try block printing over a spattered surface. Paper can also be sewn by hand or with a machine.

Quilling

Blocks of quilling papers can be purchased from most art and hobby shops. They come in a number of widths and colours. They are usually 45 cm (18 in) in length, but they can be torn or cut to specific lengths.

To make coils, as in the picture frame on page 50, you will require a quilling tool, which should be available from the same shop as the papers. If you cannot obtain one, then use a large-eyed needle or a cocktail stick with a split at the top to hold the paper while coiling.

Cut a length of quilling paper, and slip the end of the paper into the slit on the quilling tool. Proceed to coil it around the end of the tool until you reach the end of the paper, when you will be able to slip it off. The tighter you pull the paper, the tighter the coil will be.

To make a slightly different version – a scroll – repeat the instructions for the coil, but curl only half of the paper strip. Turn the strip around and curl the other half of the strip in the opposite direction.

The resulting coils and scrolls can be simply adhered into position using a clear adhesive such as PVA glue.

Quilling is an imaginative way to decorate gift boxes and greetings cards. Even a small piece of quilling can work well.

Papier mâché

Papier mâché is a time-honoured process where a number of layers of torn paper strips and adhesive are applied to a basic mould. Once dry, the papier mâché is removed from the mould to produce a replica item which is both strong and light. The piece can then be built up and decorated.

Newsprint is the most common and successful paper to use, but most other uncoated papers can be used. Flour and water, non-fungicidal wallpaper paste or even PVA glue can be used to layer the paper strips together.

An initial coating of petroleum jelly is applied to the mould to prevent it sticking. Then, once a number of layers – roughly four to five – have been applied to the mould, it is left to dry in a warm place. Once fully dry it can be eased off the mould, possibly with the additional help of a scalpel, and either more papier mâché can be added to enhance or manipulate the shape, or it can be simply sanded down and primed with a coat of white emulsion paint before decoration. A protective coat of matt, satin or gloss varnish is applied at the end.

Decoupage

This Victorian technique was originally used to adorn what might be dull, characterless furniture or household items.

It is a very simple technique which basically involves cutting up attractive pictures and images and gluing these on to a clean, grease-free, flat surface. Layers of polyurethane varnish are then applied, allowing thorough drying between each coat, until you have built up an extremely durable, glossy, decorative surface. Traditionally, many more coats of varnish were applied, but the decoupage project in this book requires only two or three.

Collage

This simple technique is employed in several of the projects.

Using a light pencil, draw your chosen shapes, or trace templates provided in the book and reproduce them on to the papers you plan to use in the collage. You may like to draw out a plan of where the shapes are to be placed on the background card or paper. Experiment with your shapes before adhering them, cutting out extra shapes if

necessary. Be sure you are happy with the composition before you embark on gluing them into position. Use PVA glue on normal papers or card, but water it down a little if you are gluing tissue papers. Apply the glue evenly, using a little square of thin card as a spreading tool; this will ensure no wrinkling or bubbling occurs.

Constructing a box

Use the measurements you have been provided with at the beginning of the project. Use a ruler and pencil to measure and draw out the required pieces of card. A strong card, mounting board or grey board are most suitable. In order to create a neat finish on the edges and a smooth-fitting lid, it is important to follow the measurements provided. Use a sharp knife or scalpel together with a steel ruler on a cutting mat or piece of scrap card. Apply adhesive to both edges that are to be joined, leave for a few minutes to become tacky and then carefully press the pieces together. Now use the same method to adhere the base to the box; repeat for the lid. Apply tape to the edges for extra support if the box is to be covered.

Other decorative details

A number of other decorative details are used throughout the book to enhance and finish certain projects; these include decorative strings, ties, cords, trimmings, dried flowers, beads, sequins, buttons, metallic wires, etc. Remember, there is no reason why you could not employ other decorative details of your own choosing to result in something more original.

> **Note:** To complete some of the projects, you will need to apply a coat of varnish to protect the item from general wear. Acrylic varnish is perfectly adequate for most pieces. Polyurethane is tougher and more durable but can yellow with age.

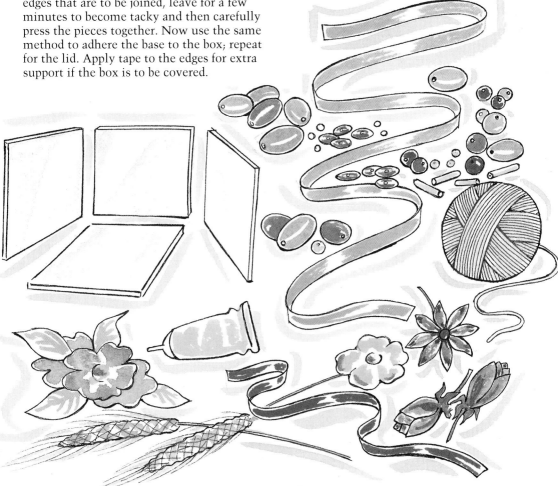

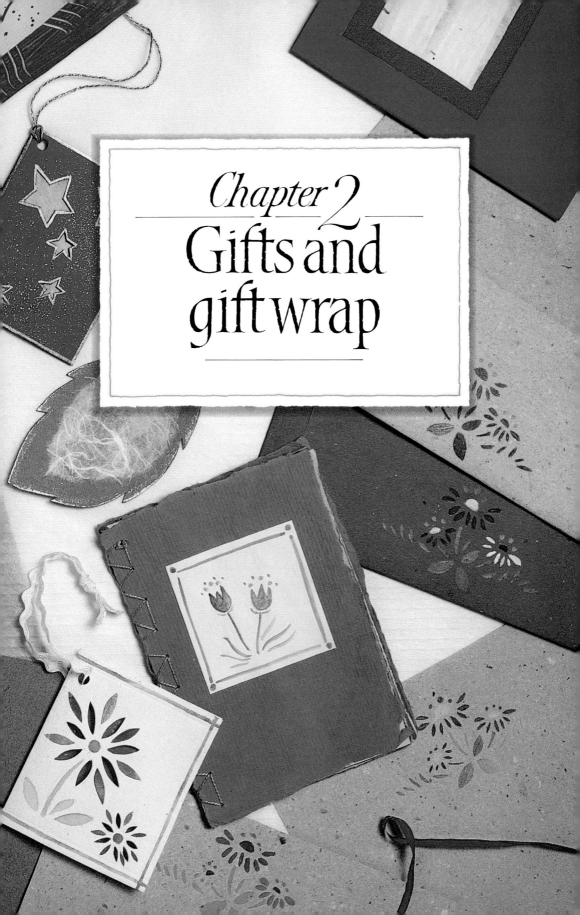

Chapter 2
Gifts and gift wrap

Gift box

This special gift box is constructed from cardboard and decorated with delicately pressed flowers, placed between layers of fine paper. Attractive ribbons, twines and trims have been added, along with a clutch of dried flowers to complete this pretty presentation box, which the recipient will no doubt want to keep along with the gift you choose to place inside.

REQUIREMENTS
Sheet of pale or pastel paper
PVA glue
Sheet of translucent paper
Pressed flowers and leaves
Greaseproof paper
Grey board or mounting board
Two different colours of tissue or metallic
*   paper*
Raffia or twine
Dried flowers
Shredded tissue

1 Take the large piece of base paper in pastel or a very pale colour and apply a layer of diluted PVA glue. Create a pleasing pattern on this with the pressed flowers and leaves. Now lay the translucent paper on top of the flowers and base paper. Cover the whole paper 'sandwich' with a sheet of greaseproof paper and press gently with a warm iron.

2 Using the measurements provided, cut out the box and lid pieces from the grey card or mounting board. Run a thin line of neat PVA glue along the two outer edges of the side pieces and along the two corresponding cut edges of the other pieces, as shown. Leave to dry for 10 minutes and then carefully press together.

3 Apply a line of glue along the edges of the base piece and along the bottom edge of the side pieces you just joined. Wait 10 minutes and attach the base piece. Repeat this procedure for the lid.

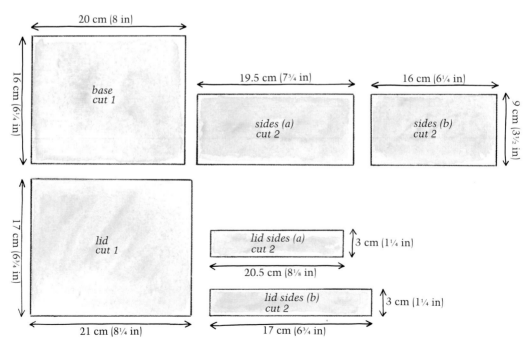

20 cm (8 in)	
base cut 1 — 16 cm (6¼ in)	19.5 cm (7¾ in) — sides (a) cut 2 / 16 cm (6¼ in) — sides (b) cut 2 / 9 cm (3½ in)
lid cut 1 — 17 cm (6½ in) / 21 cm (8¼ in)	lid sides (a) cut 2 — 3 cm (1¼ in) / 20.5 cm (8⅛ in) / lid sides (b) cut 2 — 3 cm (1¼ in) / 17 cm (6¾ in)

Gossamer-type paper encapsulates a scattering of tiny dried petals to create the covering for this attractive gift box. Use twine, raffia, ribbons or paper ribbon as a tie and a cluster of dried flowers to decorate. Inside, the box is trimmed with a dragon-tooth edging.

6 Spread PVA glue across the paper and proceed to stick all the sides and the base of the box, turning the edges over inside the box as you go. Smooth the surfaces down by using the side of your hand or a clean cloth.
7 Once all the turn-ins and overlaps are glued into place, cut and glue a piece of paper to fit in the base of the box. Repeat steps 4 and 5 to cover the lid.

4 To cover the box, it will help if you make a measuring gauge to work out the size of the paper required. All you need is two long strips of paper, one for the length and one for the width. Fold one strip around all the corners and mark on the folds with a pencil, right down to the base of the box. Repeat this for the other dimension.

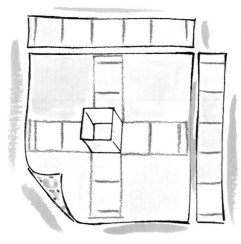

5 Now lay out the two strips on to the paper you made earlier with the flowers. Lay the box on to the paper as well. Use the measuring strips to mark out the area of paper around the box and how it will fit, as shown in the diagram. Mark out flaps and nicks to be cut away for a neat finish.

Note: Try to prevent the pressed flowers from lying on the edges or corners of the box. Keeping the flowers small and in little clumps should prevent this happening.

---

8 To make an attractive interior to the box, take two sheets of tissue or metallic paper in colours which will complement those used on the box and lid. Measure all four sides to the box, on the inside edge; mark this measurement on to the tissue/metallic paper. Cut four strips 2 cm (¾ in) wide and four in a different colour 2.5 cm (1 in) wide. Along one edge of all the strips, cut a zigzag.
9 Cut out the eight strips and glue them to the inside top edge of the box, in pairs, as shown in the photograph.
10 On the lid of the box, arrange a small decoration of dried flowers, securing them with some dabs of glue. Fill the box with shredded tissue and add the gift. Put the lid in place and tie with twine or raffia to complement the box.

Variations
If you decide that pressed flowers are not a suitable decoration for your box, there are alternative things to use. Try scraps of torn paper, fine leaves, sequins, glitter and coloured threads. You can also decorate the lid with an alternative feature.

Gift tags and labels

Tags and labels add that special finishing touch to a beautifully wrapped gift and can be designed to complement the giftwrap. Shapes can be chosen to mark the occasion for which the tag is being made, eg, a Christmas star, Valentine's heart, etc.

These tags also work out very inexpensive as they use up any scraps of paper left over from other projects. We have included cut-outs, stitching, interesting twines and ribbons along with embossed shapes to add a relief detail.

Make tags to match handmade giftwrap (overleaf) using the same decorative features. Use a variety of papers: different colours, weights and textures.

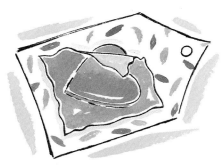

REQUIREMENTS
Scrap papers
PVA glue
Coloured twine, ribbon, etc
Variety of decorations, such as leaves,
    flowers, buttons, lace, etc
Hole punch
Hole reinforcing rings
Pinking shears

1 Collect together a number of different papers and cut out a basic tag shape: a rectangle, square, heart, circle or even an item like a leaf.

2 To emboss the tag: cut out a shape from thin board or thick paper and glue this to the basic tag. Cut or tear a shape from another piece of paper, preferably a handmade paper. Apply a coat of diluted PVA glue to this paper and dampen it slightly. Place the paper over the shape stuck to the tag and press down with a damp sponge. The shape underneath will appear quite clearly.

3 Other decorative features: try a collage of textured paper strips, glue on bits of twine, dried flowers, berries, spices, or even stitch the tag using coloured threads. Pinking shears will give you a fun edging.

4 Complete the tag by punching it with a hole, sticking a ring reinforcement on both sides and threading through matching ribbon, cord or twine.

These gift tags represent just a few designs which you can make quickly and easily. Use as many papers and trims as you can think of.

Gift wrapping paper

Designing your own decorative giftwrap gives you the chance to be bold, experimental and creative. For this project, I have given instructions for decorating your papers in a variety of ways using a number of mark-making techniques. One of the simplest methods is block printing or stamping. This method uses a variety of objects that are found around the home, such as corks, cardboard tubes and cotton reels. Spattering and combing are also included, as well as the centuries-old method of paste colouring. This last technique involves a little more preparation, time and skill, but the effects are superb.

Try decorating all types of papers: brown paper, sugar paper and even tissue paper.

REQUIREMENTS
A variety of large sheets of paper
Water-based paints and inks
Potatoes, corks, cardboard tubes, cotton reels, sponges, etc
Combs
Stiff-bristled brush or toothbrush
Flour and water

Block printing or stamping

1 The simplest method of making your own giftwrap is to employ something to act as a stamp, which can be applied with paint and stamped over the paper. Collect a number of objects, ie, corks, cardboard tubes, pieces of sponge or polystyrene and halved potatoes.
2 If you want a regular, repeating pattern, use a pencil and ruler to mark out lines for where the design will appear. Otherwise, you can stamp away in a random fashion.
3 Dip the object into a saucer of paint, blot off the excess on to scrap paper and stamp on to the paper you wish to decorate. Do

this several times until the design begins to fade; recharge the object with paint and continue until the pattern is complete.
4 Once you have completed printing with one item, you can go back with another one. For example, you could create circles using a tube and, later, go back with a sponge and make a mark in the centre of each circle.

Combing

Paint the paper with a background colour. You can wait until this has dried or work while it is still wet. Dip a comb into another colour paint and drag it across the paper, either in a straight line or in a wavy pattern. Be really experimental.

Spattering or diffusing

1 Dilute the paint to a thin consistency. Take a stiff brush or toothbrush and dip this into the paint.

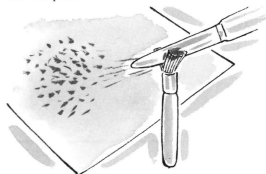

2 Hold the brush about 15 cm (6 in) from the paper. Keep the bristles upright – as shown in the illustration – and draw your finger or a blunt knife across them, towards yourself, so that a spray of paint is released from the brush and on to the paper. You can then repeat this with a different colour.

Create your own giftwrap by decorating plain sheets of paper. Bold colours and designs are achieved with block printing and paste decoration.

Paste decorating

Another interesting method of decorating a large area of paper is by using a coloured paste. This technique dates back to at least the 18th century when a mechanical press was used to print an image on to the coloured paste. It is a very simple method, yet gives outstanding results. Choose papers that are not too flimsy and avoid glossy or very absorbent papers.

1 Make up a paste by mixing together 85 g (3 oz) of plain, white flour with 500 ml (1 pt) water. Leave to stand for about 30 minutes or a little longer, then place in a double saucepan or in a heatproof bowl in a saucepan of water. Place on a low heat and gradually bring to a boil, stirring constantly. Cook for 10 minutes and allow to cool before use.

2 Divide the paste into clean jam jars or yoghurt pots and add the colours. You can use inks, powder paints or any water-based paints to colour the paste. Bear in mind the colours will dry a little paler.

3 Lay the paper you want to decorate on to a flat, newspaper-covered surface. Drizzle the coloured paste in a line along one edge of the paper and use a wide brush, such as a decorator's paste brush, to spread the mixture evenly and quite thickly over the surface of the paper, right over the edges.

Note: All the papers, however decorated, will benefit from being left to dry then placed under a weighted board (use bricks, books or cans of food as weights) for a day or so to flatten them.

4 Because the flour paste can dry quite quickly, you need to make your designs quickly, too. There are a number of different ways to do this. You can use a sponge or stiff brush to blotch and stipple a pattern across the coloured paste. Or by using combs, or small pieces of thick cardboard with a wavy or zigzag edge to drag along the paste. You can also experiment with other items to make unusual and original impressions in the paste; even your fingers can create lovely patterns.

Variations

Paste Instead of using flour to make a paste mixture, try other coarser flours, such as wholewheat flour, for a more textured finish. Or use cornflour or even non-fungicidal wallpaper paste made just a little thicker than the manufacturer recommends for a different effect.

Potatoes A flat potato half can make an abstract pattern by itself, but for something a little more interesting, carve a design into the potato. Do this by drawing a simple motif on to the cut potato. Using a craft knife, cut away the potato all around the motif, so that your device stands proud. (For more details, see page 16.)

Sketch book

The technique I have described and illustrated in this project is inspired by a Japanese method of bookbinding – sewing the layers of paper and cover together with coloured silk threads. Making your own book to use for drawing, painting or as a cuttings book makes it that much more personal and special. By including unusual handmade papers and then decorating the cover using one of the methods employed elsewhere in the book, you can achieve a very individual and beautiful gift. Choose a really special paper to serve as the cover.

Sketch and note books made in a folk-art style from a selection of papers. Stitching is used for the binding and as an embellishment.

*Sheets of handmade or watercolour papers
    in colours or natural*
Paper for cover
Long needle with large eye
3 or 4 different coloured embroidery silks
Bradawl or very sharp, long needle
*Decorative finishes, such as coloured
    threads, dried flowers, leaves or shells*
PVA glue

1 Choose what type of paper you wish to use in your sketch or drawing book. You could buy quality drawing or watercolour paper, handmade or coloured papers. I suggest a finished measurement of 28 × 22 cm (11 × 9 in). Measure and cut or tear the paper to the suggested size. Tearing the paper gives it a more natural, less severe finish. To do this, fold the paper to the suggested size, make a crease, and then tear along the crease. Repeat this until you have enough pages to fill your book; the amount required depends on how thick you want the book, and how thick the paper is that you are using. Once piled up you should end up with a depth of about 1.5–2 cm (½–¾ in).
2 Assemble the pile of paper by shaking the edges into alignment and knocking them against the flat surface of a table. They will all shift into place. Do not worry if there is a subtle difference in the sizes of the papers, this adds to the hand-crafted quality of the book. Put the pile of papers to one side.

3 Prepare a back and front cover for the book (a little larger than the paper inside), by decorating a very special piece of paper. The example here uses a three-dimensional collage technique which incorporates hand stitching and sewing buttons and cord in an attractive design. It is very simple and is all the more effective because it is worked on such a special paper. However, you could decorate your cover with a paper collage, by sticking on lace, flowers or dried leaves or by using embossing (see page 25).
4 Once you have decorated the front cover, lay the two covers on either side of the pile of papers you prepared earlier. The covers should be flush with the papers along the spine, but you should have a small overlap on the other three sides. Use a light pencil and ruler to mark a row of dots along the spine edge about 1 cm (⅜ in), and 1.5 cm (⅝ in) apart.

5 Place the stack of papers on to a piece of wood or a thick piece of card to protect the worksurface. Take a bradawl or other long sharp implement, such as a needle, and proceed to make a row of holes through all the layers of papers where marked. As you do this, wedge the papers into a corner or clamp them together to keep them as still as possible so they do not move out of alignment.
6 Thread a large needle with brightly coloured embroidery silk or thread, there is no need to knot it. Proceed to insert the needle into the first hole, leaving a longish tail, come out the other side, and bring the needle back through the next hole. Continue this running stitch until you have reached the other end of the papers. Leave a long tail at this end before cutting the thread with scissors.
7 Thread a needle in another colour embroidery thread that contrasts with the first colour.

Proceed to sew in the same way as before but begin on the other side, so the threads cross over one another. Tie the two loose threads together at each end.

Coloured embroidery thread creates a simple yet attractive binding.

8 Now thread the needle in a third colour thread, and stitch down the spine of the book using the same holes, and then back up again (using a fourth colour, if you wish) to create a zig-zag pattern.

> **Note:** *When you are at the point of sewing the pages together along the spine, you may have difficulty keeping all the pages lined up. To assist you at this stage try inserting a long glass-headed pin into each hole after you have made it. Remove the pin as you come to sew each hole.*

9 Make a slit on the edge of both covers about 1 cm (³⁄₈ in) from the edge. Insert a length of cord or ribbon into each slit and knot or glue them on the inside to hold them securely. Sew or glue a button on to the front cover and tie the cords around it to act as a decorative fastener.

Variations
When you stitch along the spine using the coloured threads, you could sew in a different stitching pattern, creating an alternative finish. It is important that, whatever stitching pattern you decide to use, the book is held securely together.

Paper jewellery

Paper has qualities that make it a practical medium for jewellery, such as its lightness, so it moves attractively and is easy to manipulate and decorate. It is also really quite durable and tough, especially if coated with a protective varnish. I have illustrated and described a couple of techniques, although you can experiment and come up with an individual creation.

REQUIREMENTS
Variety of coloured papers
Gold rubbing paste
PVA glue
Knitting needle
Sharp thick needle
Coloured tissue papers
Acrylic varnish
Coloured bead cord
Jewellery fittings

Rolled beads

1 Choose papers you are going to use to make these beads. Avoid tissue papers, but generally most papers should be fine. I have used sugar papers in contrasting colours. You can also decorate papers before cutting and rolling. Use techniques such as spattering, spraying or scribbling with crayons or felt tips; these methods are mentioned in more detail on page 17.

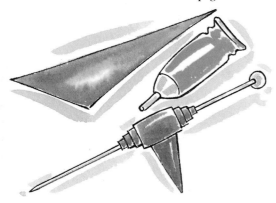

2 Use a ruler and light pencil to draw long thin triangles of different sizes and lengths but no more than about 12 × 3 cm (5 × 1¼ in). The longer the triangle, the fatter the bead, but make a variety so the beads will be more interesting. Cut these out.
3 Apply glue to one side of the triangle and proceed to roll the paper up into a hollow tube, starting at the wide end. You may find

it easier to do this over a knitting needle or something similar. Continue until you have enough beads.
4 Rub a little gold paste lightly on to the beads to give them a sparkle.

Scrunched beads

The other beads illustrated here are simply small pieces of tissue and sugar paper that have been scrunched up and rolled into a variety of different-sized balls, with a small amount of watered-down PVA glue (1:1) to hold them together. The PVA glue solution also makes them tough once dry. Once dry, a large needle is used to pierce a hole through the bead for the cord to pass through. Decorate these beads with the gold paste in the same way as the rolled beads, if you like.

Once all the adhesive is dry and the holes have been pierced, you may like to coat the beads in varnish for extra durability, either matt or gloss. Once dry, arrange the beads as you wish and thread them on to coloured cord or attach them to earring wires.

Variations

In this project I have only covered two methods of creating beads, but you could incorporate other simple ways of manipulating paper and card, such as tiny folds and fluting, and weaving paper as shown in the Christmas baskets.

> **Note:** *When coiling the long triangular strips into beads, it is important to roll with the grain of the paper. To find the grain, try tearing the paper in both directions; one way will be easier and neater; this is the direction of the grain.*

Necklaces fashioned from a selection of paper beads. A little gilt wax adds sparkle and lifts the colours of the paper.

Greetings cards

Although there is a wide variety of cards on shop shelves, the really impressive ones are also the most expensive. So why not try some of the possibilities here? I have included various methods, although the list of designs is virtually endless.

REQUIREMENTS
Variety of papers and card
Scoring bone or scissor blade
Glue
Inks
Watercolours

Folded paper card

The effectiveness of this example relies on the choice of papers and colours.

1 Cut a piece of card 16 × 22 cm (6 × 9 in). Mark the centre of the card and score down to create the fold.

2 Take a piece of attractive coloured paper – handmade paper works well here – and create a series of zigzag folds, creasing the edges firmly, so that you end up with a strip of gentle folds. Glue this on to the front of the card.

3 Measure around the folded piece and draw up a frame to this size on a piece of paper in a contrasting colour. It should be roughly 12 mm (½ in) wide all round. Stick this on to the card to frame the folded piece.

Pop-up card

1 Mark up and cut out on thin card, a rectangle measuring 15 × 36 cm (6 × 15 in). Fold the card equally into three along its length, as shown.

2 Using a craft knife, score four lines along one fold. Make the first and last cuts longer than the two cuts in the centre. Repeat this further down and on the second fold.

3 Cut a series of abstract shapes from brightly coloured paper and glue these on to the card in a random pattern.

Folded animal card

1 Cut out a piece of thin card 32 × 20 cm (12 × 8 in). Score and fold down the centre.
2 Enlarge the camel (right) and transfer on to the card. Cut out the camel, but do not cut through the top of the head or the hump where the fold lies. Cut away the unwanted card and decorate the camel with bold paints, inks, glitter, felt scraps and other decorative finishes.

Just some of the greetings cards designs you can make: a pop-up card (left), folded paper card and a camel. The camel pattern (right) is shown here half size.

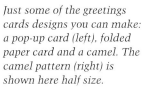

Variations

Torn paper Tear pieces of colourful tissue, and glue them overlapping on to the card. Frame as in step 3 of the folded card.

Pierced paper Draw a motif on the card, then pierce the design evenly using a large, sharp needle.

Embossed card Create an embossed motif on your card, see page 25.

Stencilled stationery

This personalised stationery makes an ideal gift for virtually anyone. The colour of paper and choice of motif you decide to stencil will determine whether the gift is for male or female, young or old.

Buying sheets of beautiful handmade or even machine-made paper which can then be cut to make writing paper and envelopes can be a pleasure in itself. But if you would rather not do this, you can decorate ready-bought plain stationery.

REQUIREMENTS
Large sheets of paper
Stencil card or acetate
Paint, printing inks or crayons
Masking tape
Stencil brush
PVA glue

1 Using a ruler and light pencil, divide the large paper into writing paper-size sheets – A4 is a good size. Cut this out using a craft knife, scalpel or, if you have access to one, use a guillotine.
2 Select one of the templates shown here to use as a stencil, or trace something you like from a book, magazine or other source. Transfer the tracing on to the stencil card or acetate and then cut the shape out carefully using a sharp craft knife and cutting mat.
3 Place the stencil on the writing paper – towards the top is a common place for a motif, although you could place it towards the bottom, or in one of the four corners. Hold the stencil in place with some masking tape.

Note: If you are new to the art of stencilling, it is probably best to practise first on scraps of paper until you are pleased with the result.

---

4 If you want to use paints for your design, mix up the colours you require and put them into some shallow containers, like saucers. Dab the stencil brush into the paint, lifting out only a small amount so that, when it is applied, it does not seep under the stencil. Apply the paint in a dabbing motion, holding the brush upright. Instead of using solid blocks of one colour, try a mixture of colours to obtain a gradated effect. (You can use crayons or even felt-tip pens rather than paints, if you wish.)
5 Carefully remove the stencil from the paper and wipe it dry so that it can be used again. If you need to add further detail to the motif, such as eyes or the middle of a flower, simply dot them in after the design has dried, using a fine paintbrush.
6 To make your own envelopes, copy the pattern supplied, and map out the measurements on to matching paper. Fold and cut where indicated and stick the sides and back together using glue. Apply a stencilled detail on the envelope; either on the flap or one of the bottom corners on either the front or the back. If you want to line the envelope, stick together two pieces of contrasting paper before cutting out. Use spray adhesive to prevent the paper warping.

Variations

If you wish to print a lot of stationery quite quickly, a block printing method may be preferable to stencilling. The easiest is potato prints. See page 16 for more details.

Beautiful handmade paper is enhanced with a simple stencilled motif. Use a variety of coloured papers, as shown here, or restrict yourself to one shade with perhaps a complementary – rather than contrasting – lining to the envelope.

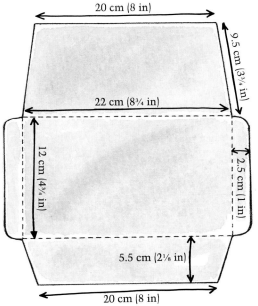

20 cm (8 in)

9.5 cm (3¾ in)

22 cm (8¾ in)

12 cm (4¾ in)

2.5 cm (1 in)

5.5 cm (2⅛ in)

20 cm (8 in)

Chapter 3
For the home

Papier mâché bowl

Papier mâché is becoming an increasingly popular craft, and a number of new and original interpretations have been created by using other materials. In this project, the basic form is removed from the mould and additional edges are added. This is combined with the application of interesting papers and touches of gold to create a primitive and exotic vessel.

REQUIREMENTS
Bowl to use as mould
Petroleum jelly
Newspaper
Flour and water paste
Sandpaper
White emulsion paint
PVA glue
Cream-coloured paint
Black felt-tip pen
Gold paint
Matt or gloss varnish

1 Cover the mould in a layer of petroleum jelly; don't smother it, but apply enough to protect the surface from moisture.

2 Tear the newspaper into a variety of small strips. Mix together flour and water in a bowl so that the mixture resembles thick batter. (See page 18 for more details.) Apply one layer of wet (not pasted) paper strips to the mould. Only after this first layer should you apply the pasted strips. This will make the removal of the papier mâché a lot easier later. Apply three or four layers of pasted strips then leave the bowl to dry in a warm place.
3 Remove the papier mâché from the mould; if no paste has touched the mould it should come away easily. If not, take a sharp knife or scalpel and make a neat cut to release it. Add more newspaper strips around the edges to create an uneven rim.

As these dry, they will bend and warp. You may also like to leave the edges torn and ragged so that these become a feature. Once you are happy with your shape, apply another one or two layers of papier mâché, smoothing it down to avoid any lumps. Leave it to dry in a warm place.
4 Once the bowl is fully dry, gently smooth the surface down with a fine grade sandpaper. Apply a coat of white emulsion paint. Once this is dry, you may like to apply a cream-coloured base coat.

5 Draw a number of simple motifs on to plain paper – following the design here – using black felt tip pen and gold paint. When dry, cut out the motifs and stick them to the bowl.
6 For extra durability, apply a coat of polyurethane varnish in either matt or gloss to the finished bowl. Clean the brush in white spirit.

Variations

Try incorporating other materials into this project, photocopied patterns, coloured mirrors and glass pieces, little gems and coloured thread, etc.

> ***Note:*** *Once the papier mâché has been removed from the basic mould it can warp because the paper shrinks as it dries, and it no longer has its mould to support it. Do not worry about this, as it actually helps to create a more naïve, quirky shape.*
>
> *It is a good idea to build up a number of layers of papier mâché – say three or four – and allow them to dry out almost completely before proceeding to apply more. This avoids possible mildew which can occur if the piece has not been allowed to dry thoroughly.*

Classical motifs border a contemporary bowl made from papier mâché. Although purely decorative, papier mâché can be wiped with a damp cloth once it has been varnished to keep dust at bay.

Tropical roller blind

Roller blind kits are easy to buy from most DIY shops and, because you are required to use your own fabric or reinforced paper, it is the perfect opportunity to design and make something to fit in a specific window.

I chose to illustrate a tropical jungle scene using rich green tissue papers and cutting away the edge to represent the luscious foliage. A splash of colour has been added by incorporating an exotic pair of love birds.

REQUIREMENTS
Roller blind kit
Large sheet of laminated/coated paper in
*   blue*
Tracing paper
Scrap card for template
Green tissue papers in various shades
Brightly coloured papers
Cord
Bead
Staple gun
Flat dowel
PVA glue
Watercolours or inks
Varnish

1 Cut a sheet of strong, preferably laminated, paper the width required to fit a specific window; read the manufacturer's instructions for the ideal measurements.
2 Use the pattern of the jungle edge and love birds and transfer these on to some scrap card to form a template around which you can draw.

A vivid jungle scene in rich greens edges a paper roller blind. When set at a window, the light will filter through and highlight the fabulous texture and colours of the papers used.

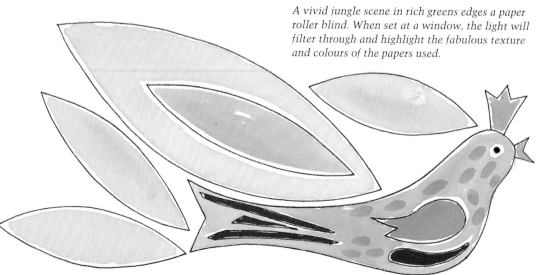

3 Transfer the jungle edge on to the bottom of the blind paper. Use sharp scissors to cut this edge away.

5 Use the card templates to draw the bird shapes on to brightly coloured paper. Draw the wings and beak in one colour and the body in another. Cut out the shapes and glue them into place. Add detail to the leaves with paints or inks.

4 Choose a variety of green tissue papers. Cut these out in various leaf shapes like those shown here, to fit over the template shape at the base of the blind paper. Use gum arabic or watery PVA glue to stick the papers to the blind.

> **Note:** You may notice when you glue the tissue papers on to the blind that slight wrinkling or warping may occur. To avoid this, place a heavy flat weight, like a large book, on to the blind between applications of the tissue papers. But place a piece of card or polythene between the design and the weight to avoid it sticking to the book.

6 Once the glue is dry, you can fit the paper to the wooden pole; attach it using a staple gun. Glue a strip of flat dowel to the back of the blind at the bottom. Attach a cord using glue and a staple to the middle of the bottom of the blind and thread on a bright bead to weight it down.

Variations
I chose to illustrate the images of the jungle, but any theme could work just as successfully, using different coloured papers; try an underwater scene, a parade of animals, letters, numbers or something more abstract.

Dressing table set

Decoupage is a Victorian craft which involves sticking cut-out paper shapes to the flat surface of a box, tray or screen. The surface is then coated with a number of layers of glossy varnish to give it a durable, lacquered finish, the paper cut-outs eventually blending in with the surface of the object being decorated.

I have employed this technique in the decoration of an attractive and practical dressing table set – two little boxes and a dish – using photocopies adhered to a distressed coloured background.

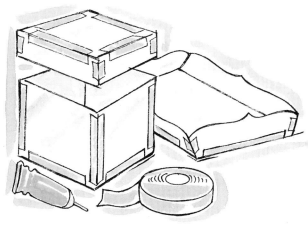

REQUIREMENTS
Tracing paper
A2 sheet of mounting board
Sticky tape or masking tape
PVA glue
Fine grade sandpaper
White matt emulsion paint
Coloured poster paints
Polyurethane varnish in satin or gloss

1 Use the cutting patterns shown here to draw up the basic patterns on to tracing paper for the boxes, lids and dish. Transfer these on to the mounting board and cut out carefully with a sharp craft knife or scalpel and a ruler. (See details on page 19 for cutting and constructing boxes.)

2 Using tape, construct the boxes, lids and dish. Use glue to stick the edges, and strengthen them with tape. Make sure you apply the tape neatly, as it may show up later when painted.

3 Apply one coat of white emulsion paint to all the pieces, both inside and out, and leave to dry thoroughly.

4 Choose two colours you wish to use as the background for the dressing table set. One colour will be applied on top of the other, with a layer of white emulsion in between. Bear this in mind when you select your colours. Apply the first colour to all the pieces, keeping the paint thick and opaque. Leave to dry.

These attractive boxes make ideal tidies for make-up, jewellery or small bottles of cosmetics.

7 Select pictures from magazines or books and photocopy them. Carefully, cut these images out, and glue them on the dressing table set in any way you choose.
8 When the glue has dried, apply two coats of glossy varnish, allowing the first coat to dry thoroughly before applying the second. Clean your brush in white spirit.

> **Note:** *The paper cut-outs can become transparent when you apply the first coat of varnish. To avoid this, apply a layer of PVA glue to the cut-outs beforehand.*

5 Apply a coat of white emulsion paint to the coloured layer and leave to dry. Finish with the second colour paint and leave this to dry thoroughly.
6 Now gently rub the surface with the sandpaper. The first colour should begin to emerge from underneath. Once you have achieved an all-over distressed effect you can begin to decorate the items.

Variations
Instead of opting for a subtle colour scheme like the one shown here, paint your background in black or scarlet and apply bold, brightly coloured pictures cut straight out of a magazine. The effect will be dazzling and exotic.

This attractive dressing table set demonstrates several paper techniques: constructing a box, creating a distressed finish and decoupage.

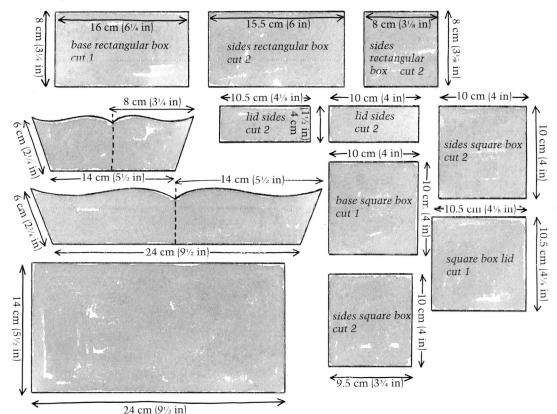

Paper lampshade

Lampshades are relatively simple items to make using a basic frame and a variety of coloured, handmade and decorative papers. Craft shops and some department stores sell basic lampshade frames; select a wide one so that the heat from the bulb has less chance of overheating the paper.

To make the very best of combining papers with light, I have cut away the shade in patterns, and applied other, brighter coloured papers on the inside, so that they glow vividly when the light is on.

REQUIREMENTS
Lampshade frame
Plain paper for pattern
Dark-coloured, strong paper
Brighter coloured, lightweight papers
Masking tape
Needle
Coloured thread
PVA glue
Strong-coloured paper for binding edges
Gold paint

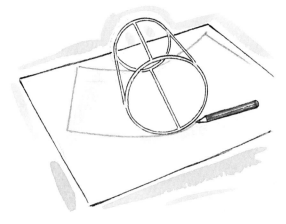

1 Place the frame on its side on the plain paper. Mark on the paper and on the frame both top and bottom. Now, gently roll the frame along the paper, marking with a pencil at the top and bottom, where it touches the paper. When you have rolled the frame right round to where you began, you will have a gently curving shape on the paper. Cut this out and use it as a template to draw around.

2 Place the template on the darker, stronger paper and draw round it, allowing an extra 2 cm (¾ in) at one end for an overlap. Cut out this shape, which forms the basic shade.

3 To make the cutaway shapes in the shade, first wrap the shade around the frame and indicate lightly in pencil where the wire bars fall. By doing this, you can avoid placing your cut-outs where the wire will show. Draw simple spiral shapes, like those shown here, on to the wrong side of the paper shade. Use a sharp scalpel or craft knife to cut out these shapes.

4 Cut pieces of bright, lightweight paper to cover the holes you have made. Glue these pieces over the holes on the wrong side of the shade. Leave to dry. If you apply a thin coat of PVA glue and water solution (1:1) to the papers, they will become taut.

5 Attach the shade to the frame using small pieces of masking tape. Apply a line of adhesive where the two edges join, and stick these together.

6 Once the shade is taped into position, thread a needle with coloured thread and sew a line of neat, long stitches that will attach the shade to the frame, all around the top. When you have been all around the top, repeat around the bottom. With the shade firmly stitched to the frame, you can remove the masking tape.

A paper lampshade is quite straightforward to make – this design is bold and modern with swirling cut-outs revealing the light through finer, translucent paper insets. A paper lampshade is perfectly safe providing you always use a low-wattage bulb. Look for lampshade frames in craft shops or department stores.

Note: Choose a thick paper as the basic shade, one that is completely opaque to make the best of the cutaway patterns. A paper that is dark on one side and pale on the other is ideal; the pale side forms the interior of the shade, thus reflecting the light and keeping the lampshade cooler.

7 To neaten the stitched edges, choose a contrasting coloured paper, cut it into strips and glue over top and bottom edges to bind them. Define the cut-outs with gold paint.

Quilled picture frame

The delicate scrolls which fill and decorate this picture frame are created using a quilling tool, which coils specially prepared strips of coloured papers. Quilling papers and tools are available from craft shops.

Choose quilling strips in any colour range you like and paint the background of the frame in a colour which will enhance them.

REQUIREMENTS
Mounting card
PVA glue
Quilling tool
Quilling papers
Poster paints
Tweezers

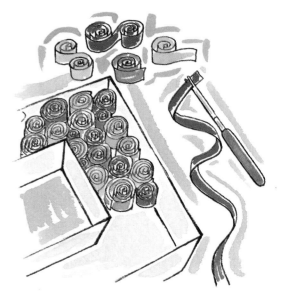

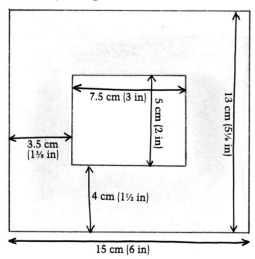

1 Draw out the basic frame on the mounting card using the dimensions shown. Cut out and construct the frame using glue to secure the joins.

2 Paint the frame in the background colour of your choice. Leave to dry. Quilling papers come in a range of colours; I have used just two, but you might like to use more.

3 Using the quilling tool, roll each strip of paper in one direction at one end, and repeat in the opposite direction at the other, as shown. Cut the papers to a variety of lengths and quill some tighter than others, and even roll some in only one direction. The more variety, the more interesting the final effect.

4 Glue the quilled papers into place using the PVA glue. Tweezers are useful to ease the scrolls into place. It does not really matter how you arrange the scrolls, but they should lie closely together, leaving no gaps.

Variations

You can create pictures from the quilled papers. By using one colour paper, form the shape of a flower or animal, then fill in the background with scrolls in another colour.

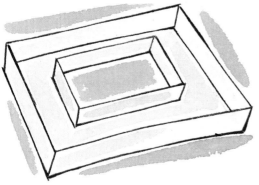

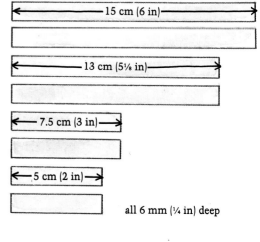

all 6 mm (¼ in) deep

The art of quilling – where delicate curlicues and scrolls are formed from paper strips by using a quilling tool – is a well-established one. Here, quilling is used to great effect to fill a quick-to-assemble picture frame with a filigree pattern in co-ordinating colours.

Note: If you cannot obtain a quilling tool easily, use a large-eyed, thick, blunt needle. You can make your own papers by cutting coloured paper into thin strips.

Star tablecloth

Customise your own party tablecloth by decorating plain paper tablecloths. These are readily available in a wide range of colours from stationers or stores selling partyware.

The design here uses two tablecloths of different colours so that you can cut out shapes on the top cloth to reveal the one underneath.

REQUIREMENTS
Blue paper tablecloth
White paper tablecloth
Stencil card
Gold glitter or spray paint
White paint
Sponge or stencil brush
Scrap card (optional)
Gold adhesive stars

1 Take the blue tablecloth and, using a ruler and pencil, draw a zigzag pattern all around the edge. Cut this out with either scissors or a craft knife.

2 Draw a simple star shape on to the stencil card. (You can trace over the one shown here and enlarge it, if you are not confident to draw your own star shape.) Using a sharp craft knife, cut out the shape. Position the stencil on to the zigzag edge of the tablecloth and sponge or brush on the white paint. (See page 16 for more details on stencilling.) Repeat this around the whole tablecloth.
3 Complete the zigzag edge on the blue tablecloth with a very light spray of gold paint, as shown.

4 When all the paint is dry, mark out a number of small stars over the blue tablecloth and in the centre of the stencilled stars. (If you are not confident to draw the stars freehand, use the pattern shown here once again. Trace the star and transfer it to a piece of scrap card. Cut this out and use it as a template to draw around.) Use a craft knife or scalpel and ruler to cut out these smaller stars.
5 Put the blue tablecloth aside and take the white one. Stick the small gold adhesive stars in a random pattern all over the white paper cloth.
6 When all the paint is dry, place the blue tablecloth over the white one at an angle to reveal the cloth beneath.

A midnight blue tablecloth glitters with stencilled and cut-out stars. It is placed over a white tablecloth sprinkled with tiny gold stars.

Seashore napkin rings

These seashore-inspired napkin rings are created using a papier mâché technique around cardboard bands. Twine has been added to the band to build up a wavy relief and the completed napkin rings are painted then highlighted with gold ink.

REQUIREMENTS
Thin cardboard
Twine and sticky tape
Flour and water paste
Sandpaper
White emulsion paint
Poster paints and gold ink
Strong, all-purpose glue and varnish

1 To make four napkin rings, draw four strips measuring 18 × 6 cm (7 × 2¼ in) on to the thin card. Cut these out using a sharp craft knife. Cut a wavy edge into both long edges of each strip. Use the templates provided to cut out two seahorses and two starfish, also from the thin card.

2 Bend each strip of card into a ring and fasten the card together with a piece of sticky tape. Tape a piece of twine in a wavy pattern around the middle of each cardboard ring as shown.
3 Make a flour and water paste (see page 40) and tear the newspaper into small strips. Paste each strip and apply to the rings; cover each one with about three to four layers.
4 Screw up small pieces of scrap paper and tape them to the cardboard starfish and seahorses. This gives the finished shapes a three-dimensional quality. Cover each shape in strips of papier mâché and leave to dry.

5 Once all the pieces are completely dry, smooth down all the surfaces with a fine grade sandpaper. Apply a coat of white matt emulsion paint and leave to dry.
6 Now you can decorate the pieces. I have chosen soft pastel colours that represent the sea, shells and shoreline. I have then enhanced the edges with a touch of gold ink. When you are happy with the decoration, stick each shape to the rings, using strong, all-purpose glue.
7 To complete each piece, coat the complete ring and added shape with matt or gloss varnish.

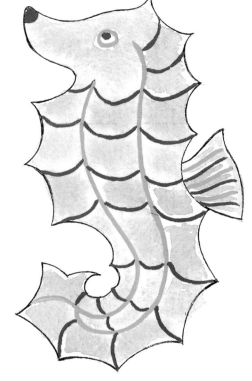

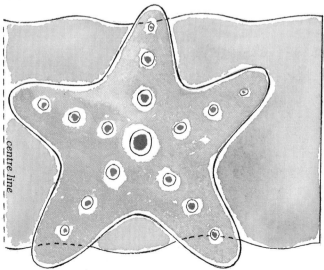

Chunky starfish and seahorses are modelled on to napkin rings made from painted cardboard.

centre line

Chapter 4
Decorations

Paper sunflowers

This bouquet of sunflowers is created with a minimum of skills from paper and florists' wire. The flowers make an artistic and unusual alternative to dried or silk varieties and, when arranged in a jug, their stunning simplicity will brighten up any corner.

To make the petals really effective, try to find tissue and crêpe paper in various shades of yellow, from light lemon to deep orange.

REQUIREMENTS
Green crêpe paper
Yellow crêpe paper
Yellow tissue paper
Needle
Strong yellow or green thread
35 cm × 1.25 mm (14 in × 1/16 in) galvanised
  wires
All-purpose glue
Florists' reel wire
Green sugar paper
Black crêpe paper
Brown crêpe paper
Corrugated card
Poster paints

1 Cut out the papers according to the measurements below:
1 × strip green crêpe paper 1 m × 15 cm (1 yd × 6 in)
1 × strip yellow crêpe paper 1 m × 14 cm (1 yd × 5½ in)
3 × strips yellow tissue paper 1 m × 15 cm (1 yd × 6 in)

2 Fold up the papers as shown and draw a line of zigzag petal shapes on each one. Continue to cut out the shapes, and unravel each length of paper.

3 Take each length of paper and layer them:
Layer 1 – green crêpe paper
Layer 2 – yellow tissue paper
Layer 3 – yellow tissue paper
Layer 4 – yellow tissue paper
Layer 5 – yellow crêpe paper

4 Using the needle and thread, sew a line of running stitches along the bottom of the layers. Gather up the papers tightly and knot them securely.

5 For the stem, take one galvanised wire and bend one end into a hook. Push the other end through the centre of the flowerhead, bend the hook once more to prevent the flower slipping off and secure the whole thing with a blob of glue.

Fabulous golden sunflowers burst from a simple pottery jug, very much in the style of Van Gogh. You will need to make at least six flowers for an effective display.

Bind the base of the flowerhead securely to the stem with a length of reel wire and tease out the petals to form a realistic flower shape.

6 Draw leaf shapes on to the green sugar paper. Give them a longish stalk as this will be used to bind them to the stem. Cut out the leaves and glue one to each stem.

7 Cover the stems with a long strip of 2.5 cm (1 in) wide green crêpe paper, winding the paper around the stem in a bandaging movement from the top to the bottom, catching in the leaf stalk as you go. Break off the paper and secure it with a dab of glue.

8 To make each flower centre, cut six to eight lengths of 30 cm × 12 mm (12 in × ½ in) black and brown crêpe paper. Cut one length of corrugated card 30 cm × 1 cm (12 in × ⅜ in). Snip into one long edge of all the strips and sandwich them together as shown. Stick each layer lightly with glue.

9 When the glue is dry, roll the layers up into a circle, using more glue to secure the roll. Ruffle the snipped edge and stick the piece into the centre of the flower.
10 To finish, paint in details such as the veins of the leaf and add stronger yellow and orange colours to make the petals more convincing.

> **Note:** *When making up the flowers, take care not to allow them to come into contact with water; even a few drops can cause the dye to run and spoil the paper. It is also advisable to keep your completed flowers away from direct sunlight as this bleaches out the colour rapidly.*

Variations
Why not study other types of similar flowers and experiment with different colours and scale but following the same basic technique. Chrysanthemums, dahlias and large daisies can work well.

Christmas crackers

Traditionally, crackers are associated with mealtimes around the festive season, but they are often found when commemorating other special occasions. The crackers I have created here are not especially in the traditional style of Christmas. With the wide variety of decorative papers and ribbons available, you can choose whatever colour or pattern you desire, whether it is for a specific occasion or just for creating something original and eye-catching to decorate your table.

By using subtle tones of blue and purple, these crackers would be appropriate for any celebration. For Christmas, you might like to try more traditional colours: green, red or gold.

Craft shops and mail order suppliers sell cracker snaps towards Christmas time, if you want to include them.

These instructions make one cracker and the box in which to present a set of them. Make as many crackers as you wish. Six to eight is a suitable number.

REQUIREMENTS
Thin card
Masking tape
PVA glue
Paper
Double-sided tape
Snaps (optional)
Scrap of cord or string
Decorative gold thread or fine cord
Giftwrap ribbon
Gold paper
Decorative cardboard for box

1 Take three pieces of card for the inner tubes (two 8.5 × 18 cm/3½ × 7 in and one, 12 × 18 cm/4¾ × 7 in). Roll up to a diameter of 5 cm (2 in), overlap and tape together.

Note: You must use a strong paper, but this does not mean the paper need be thick. Some papers are deceptively fine yet appear very fine.

To save making the tubes to fit inside the crackers cut up the cardboard tubes found in the middle of rolls of kitchen paper.

2 Position the three tubes along the bottom edge of one of the large pieces of paper. Place the longer tube in the centre between the two shorter ones. Each of the end tubes should be positioned 1.5 cm (⅝ in) from either edge of the paper, as shown. Stick the tubes to the paper with double-sided tape.
3 Insert your gift and/or snap into the middle tube. Roll the paper around the three card tubes, with an overlap of about 1 cm (½ in) and secure with double-sided tape. Turn the excess paper at the ends under and glue them down.

4 Cut two lengths of gold string or thread and leave to one side. Cut another length of soft cord or string and wrap it around the tubeless gaps on either side of the middle tube. Pull these cords gently so as not to tear the paper. Now remove the cord and tie the decorative gold thread in its place.
5 Cut a number of lengths of giftwrap ribbon, tear it lengthways and tie these around the crackers, as shown. To curl the ribbons, scrape the length of the 'tails' with one of the scissor blades.

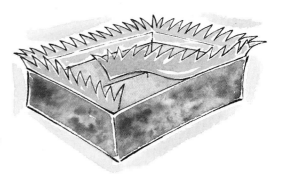

6 To make the rosettes that decorate the crackers, take a length of gold paper measuring about 16 × 2 cm (6¼ × ¾ in), now pleat the paper evenly, curve the strip into a circle and glue the two ends together. Once the glue is dry, stick each rosette on to a piece of gold or coloured paper and cut around it. Now attach to the cracker, and repeat for the others.

7 The box is simply made using decorative cardboard, but you could paint or cover plain cardboard. To make up the box use the measurements provided and draw the shape – enlarged – on the card you wish to use. Now cut this out using a craft knife and score the corners with the back of the blade. Glue the box together.

8 To decorate the edge of the box, simply cut four strips of gold paper to fit along each edge and cut a dragon tooth pattern along each one. Now glue into position.

Variations
Decorations: There is no limit to the variety of colours you can use when making up your crackers, and you can decorate them using a variety of materials, ie, dried flowers, whole spices, such as cinnamon sticks or star anis, sweets or fabric trims.
Children's names: Homemade crackers would be great at a children's party; each one could hold the name of the child and they could be decorated with simple animal or circus cut-outs.

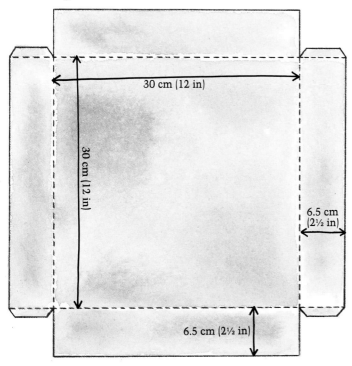

30 cm (12 in)

30 cm (12 in)

6.5 cm (2½ in)

6.5 cm (2½ in)

Paper butterflies

Coloured inks and layout paper work well together to create delicately creased and toned papers. Butterflies are an ideal subject matter to illustrate three-dimensionally, using these papers. Enhanced with glistening glass beads and a little paint, they could make a delicate addition to a dried flower arrangement or you could even use them as the basis for a mobile.

REQUIREMENTS
3–4 sheets of A4 layout paper
Variety of coloured inks
Thin cord
Thin, coloured wire
Paper glue
Watercolours or poster paints
All-purpose glue
Glass beads

1 Coat the sheets of paper with plain water, screw each piece into a ball, and then gently unfold them.
2 Choose a number of coloured inks and, using a large, wet brush, apply a thin wash of ink to each sheet. Leave the paper to dry by pegging them on to a line of string.
3 Trace the butterfly templates provided, and transfer them on to the coloured papers. You will need two sets of wings for each butterfly (one small and one large), in contrasting colours.

Note: If you do not feel confident enough to paint the patterns on to the butterflies by hand, simply cut out spots and stripes from coloured paper and stick them to the wings and body with paper glue. You could also glue on sequins and glitter.

4 Pair up the sets of wings and glue them together by running a line of paper glue down the middle. Trace the simple body shape and transfer this on to thin card. Cut out the shape and glue into position.
5 Now add painted details to the butterflies, for example stripes down the body section and dots and blobs to the wings. Use a detailing brush for precision.
6 Using the all-purpose glue, apply glass beads to the wings, to add sparkle.

7 To make the antennae, cut two pieces of coloured wire about 5 cm (2 in) long. Make two holes in one end of the body section and apply a blob of glue into each hole. Insert the wires into the holes and bend the ends underneath neatly. Thread a bead on to each wire and bend the wire to secure the bead.

A clutch of colourful butterflies adorn a potted plant. Use to enhance table decorations, a child's bedroom or to embellish a sheer curtain.

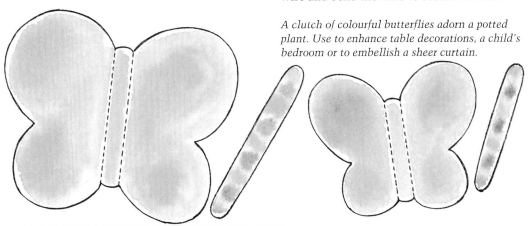

Christmas bunting

Every year at Christmas, when we embark
on decorating our tree, the same old
decorations appear, including armfuls of
tinsel. In this project, I have illustrated how
to create a very different, yet simple
decoration, to dress your Christmas tree.
The bunting is made from scraps of paper,
with decorative cord, dribbles of paint,
beads, glitter and sequins. This bunting
project would be a great one to undertake
with a group of children.

REQUIREMENTS
Paper in different colours and textures
Poster paints
Coloured decorative string, thread or cord
Paper glue
Glitter, beads, sequins

1 First, prepare the papers to make your
bunting. Because you use such small pieces
of paper, scraps you may have to hand may
need enlivening with a little paint, etc. One
way to decorate plain paper is to spatter a
variety of colours on to it. (See page 17 for
more details on paint techniques.)

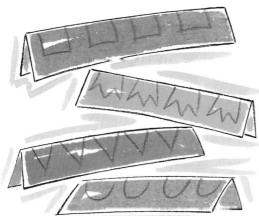

2 Once the chosen papers are ready, cut
then fold them lengthways into pieces
measuring roughly 7 × 30 cm (3 × 12 in).
Draw simple shapes on to the folded edge of
the papers, as shown. As long as they are
fairly bold, any shape can be used. Cut out.
3 Gather a number of lengths of decorative
cord, or paint string with gold paint or any
bright colour. Apply glue on to the inside of
the folded shapes and stick them on to the
cord or string, positioning them at different
intervals, alternating shapes and colours.

4 To make the bunting festive, glue
sequins, glitter or glass beads to the paper.

Ring the changes with a different tree decoration; this Christmas bunting, made from foil and paper scraps, is reminiscent of strings of popcorn in the traditional American style.

Note: *You do not need to buy any paper specially for this project; keep costs to a minimum and use old paper bags, newspapers, old giftwrap, even packaging materials. For the thread, any sort of cord, string or twine would be suitable. You can always colour it if it is dull.*

Variations

The bunting would look great at a party, festooning the room, or suspended over the buffet table. Enlarge the scale a little; even write names or a message on the flag pieces to add that personal touch.

Woven tree decorations

Weaving is a great way of combining different types of paper and varying colours, textures and thicknesses. Almost any type of paper can be woven; old paper bags, giftwrap, brown paper, tissue, crêpe, metallic and sugar papers, even old magazines or books. The more variety of colours and textures you use, the more vibrant and eye-catching the final effect will be. In this project I have shown how to turn sheets of woven paper into attractive heart-shaped Christmas tree decorations and baskets which can hold special sweets and small gifts.

REQUIREMENTS
*Papers in varying colours and textures (see
    above)*
Sticky tape
Strong paper glue
Scrap paper
Thin card
*Sweets and coloured shredded tissue
    (optional)*

To weave the paper:
1 Gather together a selection of papers you wish to weave. You may like to stick to a particular colour scheme, or simply use whatever comes to hand. Use a variety of textures and types of paper for a more interesting result. Cut the papers into strips about 1 cm (⅜ in) wide by 20–25 cm (8–10 in) long. Use a metal ruler and sharp scalpel or craft knife on a cutting mat, for the best results.
2 Take a piece of sticky tape, about 25 cm (10 in) long, stick the tape to your work-surface, or on to a piece of paper, so that the sticky side is facing upwards. Turn about 1 cm (⅜ in) of the ends under so they stick to the paper or surface. Now proceed to attach the paper strips to the sticky tape, keep them very close together and fill up the whole length of tape, varying the types of paper as you go.

> **Note:** *Although I suggest using a variety of papers in this project, be careful about using very delicate ones, as they are inclined to tear. Avoid paper that is thicker than that used for cereal boxes; it will not be sufficiently flexible.*

3 Now take more paper strips and begin to weave them through the ones you have attached to the tape. Keep them taut and close together, alternating the colours and textures as you go. Once you have reached the end of the strips and can add no more, place a strip of sticky tape at the bottom of the woven papers.

Paper hearts:
1 Trace the heart pattern left and transfer it to a piece of scrap paper. You will need two paper hearts for each decoration, so prepare as many as you wish to make. (If you want to make a number of decorations, then make a larger sheet of woven paper.) Cut out the paper hearts, and glue them to the woven paper. Leave the glue to dry.

2 Cut around the heart shapes. Apply glue on to the edges of the hearts only, leaving a gap of about 3 cm (1¼ in). When the glue has dried, pad out the hearts with little scraps of paper and glue the gap together.

Woven hearts and baskets are an excellent way to use up leftover pieces. Fill them with shredded tissue and tiny sweets or a luxury chocolate.

3 Cut two strips of paper, in any type you wish (I have used foil paper), the length of one side of the heart. These should measure about 2 cm (¾ in) wide. Using the glue, stick a strip around the edge of the heart, as shown. This will neaten the edges as well as becoming a decorative feature in its own right. You will need to make small folds in the paper strips when gluing them around the acute curves of the hearts.

4 To make the loops, simply cut two lengths of paper in contrasting colours, about 15 cm (6 in) in length, although make one strip one-third the width of the other one, ie, 2 cm (¾ in) and 6 mm (¼ in). Using a scalpel or craft knife, gently cut slits into the wider strip, approximately every 1 cm (⅜ in). Now weave the narrower paper strip through the length of the wider one. Trim any rough ends, fold over into a loop, and glue to the back of the heart at the top.

Woven baskets:
1 Follow steps for weaving paper, overleaf. Now use the pattern supplied and transfer it to a piece of thin card. Cut out the pattern and glue it to the woven paper. When the glue is dry, cut out the piece and curl it into a cylinder shape. Secure with a piece of sticky tape.

2 Place the upright cylinder on to a scrap of card and draw round it with a pencil. Remove the cylinder and draw another circle, about 6 mm (¼ in) outside the first one. Cut this shape out.
3 Make small cuts to the inner line, as shown, to make tabs. Bend these inwards. Now apply glue to the tabs and slot into the cylinder, pressing the tabs in place. Allow to dry thoroughly.

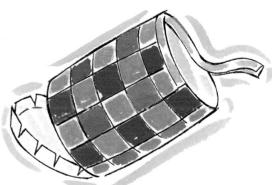

4 Cut two strips of paper, long enough to go around the top and bottom edge of the basket and about 2 cm (¾ in) wide. Glue the paper strips along the top and bottom edge of the box to neaten the edges.
5 To make the basket handles, follow step 4 of the woven hearts, and glue the paper strips inside the box on opposite sides.

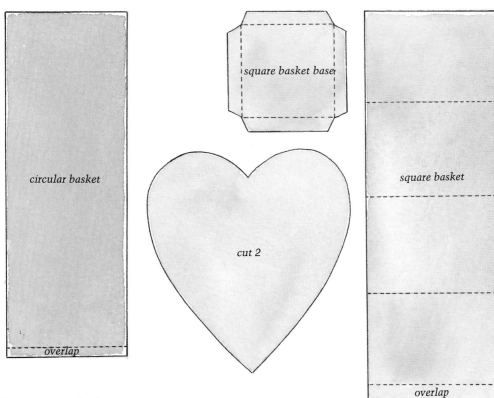

circular basket

overlap

square basket base

cut 2

square basket

overlap

Woven square baskets

These are made in a similar way to both the hearts and the circular baskets. Cut out the patterns, marking in pencil the dotted lines which indicate the folds. Glue the patterns to a sheet of woven paper. When dry, cut out the pieces. Fold the sides, as indicated, and glue along the overlap. Slot in the base, applying glue to the long tabs. Press firmly in place.

Variations

● Instead of cutting all the strips to the same width, why not experiment with different widths. The effect could be quite interesting and abstract.

● Keep to a two-tone colour scheme; an example is the crisp, clean-looking decoration in red and white, inspired by Scandinavian tree ornaments.

● Decorate the paper with paint before cutting it into strips. Try spattering with brightly coloured or metallic paint.

● Make the tree decorations in shapes other than hearts. Suggestions include other simple bold shapes, like diamonds, or, if you feel really ambitious, try making simple animal shapes.

Chapter 5
For children

Nest of boxes

Most children love to stash little treasures away in secret places. This bright and cheerful nest of boxes makes the perfect store for children's bits and bobs.

The boxes are made in strong, contrasting colours and a simple trim has been added along the edge of every box and lid to neaten the edges and add more colour. To complete the nest, a number of simple farm animal templates have been supplied to help you decorate the sides and lids.

REQUIREMENTS
A2 sheet of mounting board
Masking tape
10 sheets of brightly coloured paper
PVA glue
Stencil card
Poster paints or coloured pencils
Artists' or small household sponge

1 Using the measurements shown here, draw the box pieces on to the mounting board with a ruler and pencil. Cut out the pieces with a very sharp craft knife on a cutting mat. Mark the box pieces in pencil to indicate which piece is which; this will make it easier when you assemble them.

2 Construct the boxes by sticking the pieces together with masking tape.

Note: *When gluing the coloured paper to the boxes, make sure you apply the glue right up to the edges to ensure there are no gaps which could become dog-eared.*

Another important factor for complete success is to be very accurate with your measurements from the beginning.

---

3 Use the same measurements in step 1 to mark out the box pieces on to the coloured papers. As you will want to line the boxes in a different colour to that on the outside, mark out more shapes on contrasting coloured papers. Cut all these pieces out and glue them into place.

4 Cut out the edging strips in contrasting colours: purple, green, yellow, pink and blue. Glue the strips along all the edges of the boxes and their lids. These will neaten the edges as well as adding a finishing decorative flourish.

A delightful family of colourful boxes which will enthral most children. As long as you make these accurately according to the measurements, each box will fit snugly into its larger neighbour. You will find these boxes are ideal for storing children's treasured belongings.

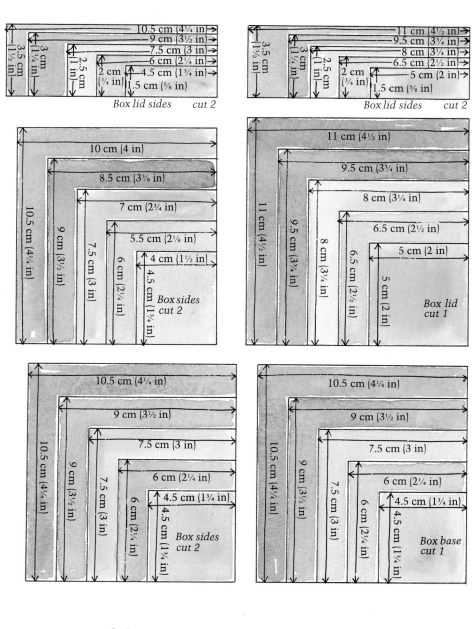

10.5 cm (4¼ in)
9 cm (3½ in)
7.5 cm (3 in)
6 cm (2¼ in)
4.5 cm (1¾ in)
1.5 cm (⅝ in)
3.5 cm (1½ in)
3 cm (1¼ in)
2.5 cm (1 in)
2 cm (¾ in)

Box lid sides   cut 2

11 cm (4½ in)
9.5 cm (3¾ in)
8 cm (3¼ in)
6.5 cm (2½ in)
5 cm (2 in)
1.5 cm (⅝ in)
3.5 cm (1½ in)
3 cm (1¼ in)
2.5 cm (1 in)
2 cm (¾ in)

Box lid sides   cut 2

10 cm (4 in)
8.5 cm (3⅜ in)
7 cm (2¾ in)
5.5 cm (2⅛ in)
4 cm (1½ in)
10.5 cm (4¼ in)
9 cm (3½ in)
7.5 cm (3 in)
6 cm (2¼ in)
4.5 cm (1¾ in)

Box sides
cut 2

11 cm (4½ in)
9.5 cm (3¾ in)
8 cm (3¼ in)
6.5 cm (2½ in)
5 cm (2 in)
11 cm (4½ in)
9.5 cm (3¾ in)
8 cm (3¼ in)
6.5 cm (2½ in)
5 cm (2 in)

Box lid
cut 1

10.5 cm (4¼ in)
9 cm (3½ in)
7.5 cm (3 in)
6 cm (2¼ in)
4.5 cm (1¾ in)
10.5 cm (4¼ in)
9 cm (3½ in)
7.5 cm (3 in)
6 cm (2¼ in)
4.5 cm (1¾ in)

Box sides
cut 2

10.5 cm (4¼ in)
9 cm (3½ in)
7.5 cm (3 in)
6 cm (2¼ in)
4.5 cm (1¾ in)
10.5 cm (4¼ in)
9 cm (3½ in)
7.5 cm (3 in)
6 cm (2¼ in)
4.5 cm (1¾ in)

Box base
cut 1

5 Trace off the farm animal templates and transfer on to the stencil card. Using a sharp craft knife or scalpel carefully cut around the shapes on the card; push the shape out to leave a stencil.

Use bold and bright papers in vivid, contrasting colours to cover, line and edge each box. One sheet each of say four or five colours should be sufficient to cover the set.

6 Mix up a selection of paints. Tape the stencil to the side of the box and begin sponging on the colour using an artist's sponge. (For more details on stencilling, see page 16.) Repeat the design on the lid and elsewhere on the box. Alternatively, fill in images with coloured pencils. Crayon in one direction only for a neat result.

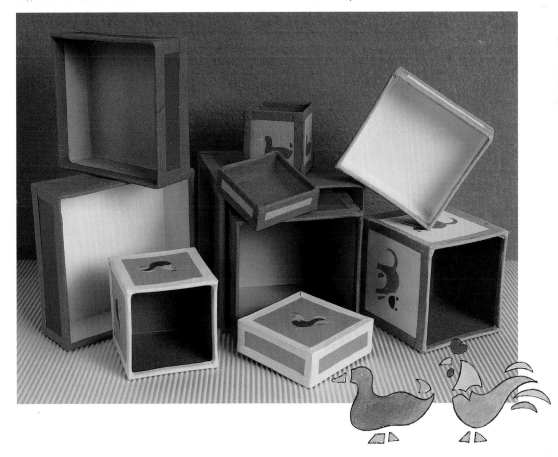

Noah's ark wallhanging

This colourful paper collage, illustrating pairs of animals walking into Noah's Ark, is a very simple project that would be ideal to make with a child. It simply involves cutting and sticking different coloured papers to build up the animals' various markings and features. Have to hand papers in as many colours as you can. A good selection includes orange, yellow, brown, black, pink, green, white and purple.

REQUIREMENTS
Blue thin card measuring 90 × 45 cm (36 × 18 in)
Paper in a wide colour range
Tracing paper
PVA glue

Most children love the challenge of collage, and the simple shapes in this jolly portrayal of Noah's ark are so straightforward that even small hands should be able to tackle them with little difficulty.

1 Using a ruler and craft knife, cut out a piece of blue card to the recommended size.
2 Cut four strips of yellow or orange paper to measure the length of each edge of the blue card; make them 4 cm (1½ in) wide. Using a light pencil, draw a zigzag pattern along each strip, but do not take the zigzag right across to one edge. Now cut these out so you have four strips of dragon-teeth.
3 Glue these strips along each edge of the blue card, as shown, so the blue card underneath creates a triangle pattern.

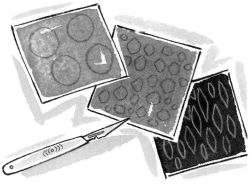

4 Enlarge the animals and ark pieces from the patterns given overleaf. Transfer two of each animal on to the coloured papers: giraffes on yellow, elephants on grey, birds on red, etc. Now transfer the ark on to brown paper and the grass on to green. Cut out all of these shapes.

5 Stick the animals on to the blue card in pairs, overlapping them in some cases, to provide a jolly, meandering queue.

6 Add the markings to the animals and the ark, as shown, by drawing the various shapes on to appropriate coloured papers. Cut these out and glue them into position.

Variations

This simple collage technique is the basis of a number of projects illustrated in this book. There is no end to the alternative pictures you could create using the technique and processes described here. Especially successful with the wallhanging idea are rows of animals, letters, numbers or even a well-cultivated flowerbed!

Sun, moon and star mobile

Crinkled layout paper, washed in diluted inks, is torn into strips and then wrapped over card shapes. These represent the sun, moon and stars which make up this mystical, planetary mobile. A fine splashing of coloured inks, combined with gold highlighting and watercolours, completes the detail, while gold-sprayed twigs are used to suspend the celestial bodies.

REQUIREMENTS
Layout paper
Coloured inks
Mounting card
PVA glue
Poster paints
Paper clips
Gold spray paint or gilt wax
3 or 4 twigs or small sticks
Gold thread

1 Crumple the layout paper to crease it; smooth it out and wash it with well-diluted coloured inks. Hang up the paper to dry.
2 Use the patterns provided to draw a sun, moon and stars on to the card. Cut the shapes out with a sharp craft knife.
3 Mix the PVA glue with water (roughly 1:1). To form the contours of the faces on the sun and moon, screw up small pieces of layout paper and glue these to make cheeks, eyebrows, etc, as shown here. When the features are formed, tear up strips of the coloured layout paper and glue the strips across all the shapes on both sides, covering the built-up areas and all the card. Leave to dry in a warm place.

4 Select the paints to colour the shapes. Use a variety of soft paintbrushes; thinner ones to paint the eyes, and thicker ones with watery paints to help blend in the features. You may also like to use gold paint to highlight the edge of the shapes; spattering with a fine spray of coloured ink can also look effective.

5 To make the hanging loops, cut the paper clips in half, as shown, using pliers. Make two holes at the sides of the sun, moon and stars with a needle. Place a blob of glue into each hole and insert the hanging loop you have just made.

6 Spray the sticks or twigs with gold paint and leave to dry. Cut lengths of gold thread and attach the stars, moon and sun in whichever way you wish to the golden twigs.

Bobbing on golden sprays, these glittering and friendly shapes will delight older children (and adults!). Made from crinkled paper strips and cardboard, this mobile gives you a great opportunity to use up scraps.

Fish kite

This simple windsock-style kite was inspired by the fish kites traditionally found in the Far East.

A length of garden wire is inserted around the mouth of the fish to help allow the wind to pass through the centre of the tube-like shape. The fish has been decorated with delicately splashed tissue papers and gold paint, to create a sparkly and aquatic effect. The fish kite is attached to a stick or rod by means of a length of string or cord.

REQUIREMENTS
Layout paper
Poster or watercolour paints
50 cm–1 m (½–1 yd) 2–3 mm (⅛ in) garden
  wire
Coloured tissue papers
Gold paint
PVA glue
String or strong cord
Rod or stick

1 Cut out two pieces of layout paper in the shape suggested here (you will have to enlarge the shape, using the enlargement facility on a photocopier). It is up to you how large to make it. I suggest about 45–50 cm (18–20 in) long. Also cut out the fins. Now wash over the shapes with diluted poster or watercolour paints in contrasting colours.

2 Glue the fins on to the inside of one of the fish shapes – just inside the edge of the fish on the top and bottom. Now place a line of glue along the top and bottom of the fish. Stick together, leaving the mouth and tail open. You will end up with a tube.

3 Bend the wire into a circle that will fit into the mouth of the fish; once you have achieved the correct circumference, secure the wire circle with tape and insert it into the mouth. Turn the paper edge inwards to cover the wire and glue it down.

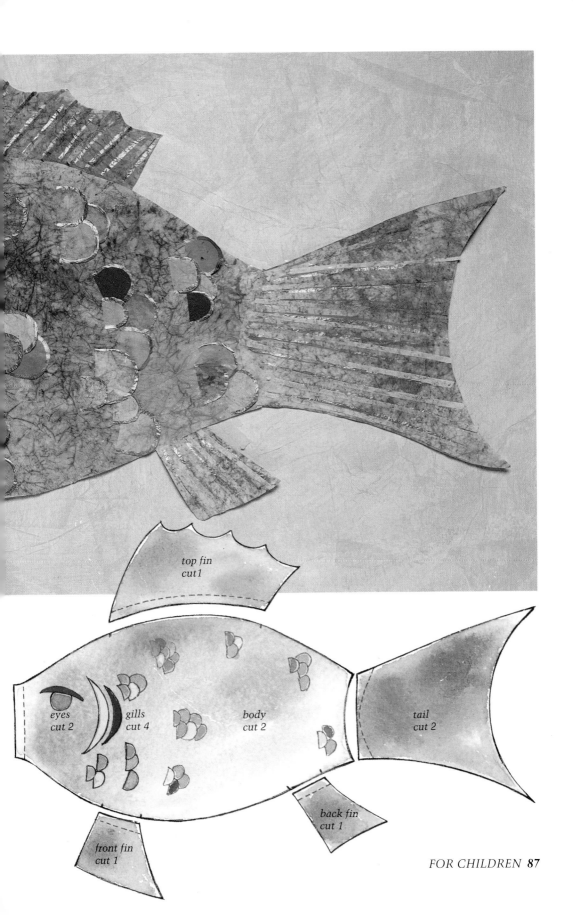

top fin
cut 1

eyes
cut 2

gills
cut 4

body
cut 2

tail
cut 2

back fin
cut 1

front fin
cut 1

4 To make the scales, take a variety of different coloured tissue papers and layout paper and spatter them with coloured and gold paint. Once dry, cut out a number of small semi-circles for the scales. You may like to edge the scales with extra gold or coloured paint to enhance their shape.
5 Now glue the scales randomly over the sides of the fish shape.
6 To complete the decoration of the fish, draw eyes, fin and tail lines, also gills, on to coloured tissue paper; cut these out and stick to both sides of the fish.

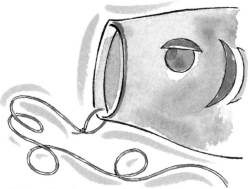

7 Attach a long length of string or strong cord to the lip of the fish by making a small hole near the wire frame, and tie the other end of the string to a rod or stick. The kite will now blow in a good wind, but it also makes a wonderful feature for a wall.

> **Note:** Because this project involves using fine, thin papers, it is a good idea to avoid handling them when they are wet, ie, after painting or spattering. It is worth hanging them on a small line until they are fully dry and therefore stronger.

Child's portfolio

This aquatic portfolio – with its bright and colourful fish – gives children a special way to store their drawings and paintings. Layout paper has been delicately washed with watery colours to create an ocean effect. Collage is combined with freehand painting and a combing technique to complete this underwater composition.

REQUIREMENTS
2 sheets A3 mounting board or thick
* cardboard*
4 sheets A3 layout paper
3 sheets A3 orange layout paper
Scraps of layout paper for bubbles
PVA glue
Tracing paper
Scrap card for templates
Plastic hair comb
Coloured inks
Fabric-based sticky tape or book cloth
* about 6 cm (2¼ in) wide*
2.5 m (2¾ yd) fabric tape about 1.5 cm
* (⅝ in) wide*
Watercolour varnish

1 Paint the two sheets of layout paper with a watered-down blue paint. Apply the paint using a fairly large brush so that you achieve a watery, almost blotchy, effect.
2 Once the paper is fully dry, trim 2 cm (¾ in) off one shorter edge and cover it completely with glue on the wrong side. Stick it to the card, matching up the three edges, and leaving 2 cm (¾ in) of card uncovered. You may get a few creases, but do not worry, as long as the paper is tightly glued to the card. Repeat this step with the other piece of blue paper and card.

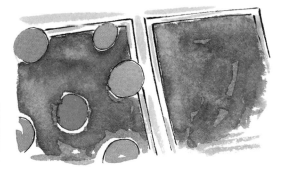

3 Paint more layout paper with a contrasting blue paint. Leave this to dry, then cut out a variety of circular shapes to form the bubbles. Stick these circles in a random pattern on each piece of paper-covered card to form bubbles.

4 Take another two sheets of layout paper, wash with orange and yellow paints. Now dip the comb into bright, contrasting orange or red paint and drag it down one of the papers to create rows of lines. Leave to dry.

5 Trace the fish templates, shown overleaf, and transfer them on to the scrap card. Cut these shapes out and use them to draw around to create 12 fish. On the plain yellow or orange paper, mark out 12 fish bodies; on the combed paper, you will need to draw 12 large fins, 24 smaller fins and 12 tails. Cut all these shapes out.

This little fish can be traced, transferred to card and used as a template for decorating the portfolio.

6 Now glue the fish bodies, fins and tail on to the portfolio card, on top of the blue patterns. Follow the illustrations as a guide.
7 Use a fine brush to add detail to the fish, ie, eyes, gills and little triangles on the bodies, to represent the scales. Paint these in a colour that will stand out well against the orange. Try green, purple or pink.

8 Stick two of the orange pieces of paper to the back of each portfolio board. Now cut the other orange paper into strips to cover the four edges. The strips for the three outer edges should be 4 cm (1½ in) wide and for the inside edge, 6 cm (2½ in). Fold the strip lengthways, creasing firmly, and glue over each edge to give a neat finish.

> **Note:** *You may find when paint comes into contact with the paper and cardboard that it encourages them to warp or crinkle. If this does happen, you can place the board or paper between two pieces of clean paper and then under a heavy weight while it is still damp.*

9 Cut a length of the sticky, wide tape a little longer than the depth of the portfolio board. Lay the tape down on your worksurface, sticky side up. Place the two portfolio boards with patterned sides facing up on to the tape neatly, so the edges are about 1 cm (⅜ in) apart. Fold down the overlap at each end and stick into place.

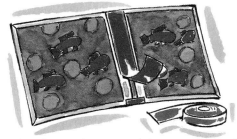

10 Take another strip of tape measuring the depth of the boards. Stick this down the join to cover it neatly. The two pieces of board are now securely joined.
11 To make ties for the portfolio, cut small slits into the top and sides of each part of the portfolio, as shown, using a sharp craft knife or scalpel.

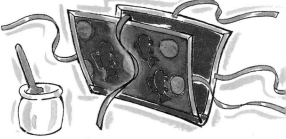

12 Cut the narrow fabric tape into six lengths. Insert the tape into the slits, leaving a little on the inside which can be glued to prevent the tapes from slipping through. If you wish to make the portfolio a little more durable, apply two coats of watercolour varnish.

Variations:
I thought this paint technique was perfect to recreate an underwater scene, but you may like to do something different. Why not get the children involved in a new design: a jungle, circus or fairground, for example.

Ideal for storing drawings or school work, this lovely aquatic portfolio is great fun to make.

Further reading

Bawden, Juliet. *The Art & Craft of Papier Mâché*. Mitchell Beazley, 1990.

Frank, Vivien. *Decorative Paper Crafts*. Letts, an imprint of New Holland, 1991.

Haines, Susanne. *Papier Mâché*. Letts, an imprint of New Holland.

Owen, Cheryl. *The Creative Book of Paper Crafts*. Salamander Books, 1990.

Shannon, Faith. *Paper Pleasures*. Weidenfeld & Nicolson, 1987.

Williams, Melanie. *Making Your Own Papier Mâché*. New Holland, 1995.

Useful addresses

Stationers and art shops should supply virtually everything you need to make all the projects in this book. Varnish and white emulsion paint are readily available in any DIY or hardware store.

United Kingdom

Paperchase
213 Tottenham Court Road
London W1A 4US
Tel: 0171 580 8496

T N Lawrence & Son Ltd
117–119 Clerkenwell Road
London EC1 5BY
Tel: 0171 242 3534

W H Smith
(Head office)
Greenbridge Road
Swindon SN2 3LD
Tel: 01796 616161
(*branches throughout the country*)

Arjo Wiggins Fine Papers Ltd
130 Long Acre
London WC2E 9AL
Tel: 0171 379 6850

Winsor and Newton
Whitefriars Avenue
Harrow HA3 5RH
Tel: 0181 424 3200
and
51 Rathbone Place
London W1P 1AB
Tel: 0171 636 4231

Australia

Artwise
13 Wilson Street
Newtown
NSW 2042
Tel: (02) 519 8234

Wills Quills
164 Victoria Avenue
Chatswood
NSW 2067
Tel: (02) 411 2627

The Paper Merchant
316 Rokeby Road
Subiaco
WA 6008
Tel: (09) 381 6489

Oxford Art Supplies
221 Oxford Street
Darlinghurst
NSW 2010
Tel: (02) 360 4066

New Zealand

Faze Papers
32 Alfred Street
Onehunga
Tel: (09) 622 2220

BJ Ball Papers
395 Church Street
Penrose
Tel: (09) 579 0059

Rosehill Paper Supplies
Bremmer Road
Drury
Tel: (09) 294 7506

The Paper House
7 Carmont Place
Mt Wellington
Tel: (09) 276 2683

Bostick NZ Ltd
78 Leonard Street
Penrose
Tel: (09) 579 9263

Index